THE POWER
OF THE
CROSS

Published in Nashville, Tennessee, by Thomas Nelson, Inc.,

The Bible version used in this publication is THE NEW KING JAMES VERSION. Copyright © 1979, 1980, 1982, Thomas Nelson, Inc., Publishers.

Library of Congress Cataloging-in-Publication Data

Stanley, Charles F.
The power of the cross / Charles Stanley.
        p. cm.
    Includes index.
    ISBN 0-7852-7065-5 (hard)
    1. Christian life—Meditations. I. Title.
BV4501.2.S719344   1998
242—dc21   97-28983
                                                            CIP

Printed in the United States of America

4 5 6 QBK 03 02 01 00

THE POWER
OF THE
CROSS

CHARLES
STANLEY

THOMAS NELSON PUBLISHERS
Nashville • Atlanta • London • Vancouver

CONTENTS

INTRODUCTION

The Cross is the cornerstone of our faith. It is the source of our healing and our hope. Through the Cross God has provided all we need for the life of godliness. In fact, the apostle Paul stated, "I determined not to know anything among you except Jesus Christ and Him crucified" (1 Corinthians 2:2).

My call to the ministry and the ongoing commitment to serve our Lord over the years came to me because of the sacrifice of Calvary. Motivation for service and sacrifice stems from our awareness of Christ's service and sacrifice: "The Son of Man did not come to be served, but to serve, and to give His life a ransom for many" (Matthew 20:28).

In the pages of this book you will see that there is power in the Cross and that this "wonder-working power" is made available to all of us through our heavenly Father's grace. He gives to us freely out of His storehouse of love, and nowhere is this love more clearly demonstrated than at the Cross.

Resting

Secure in

Your

Salvation

Blessed be the God and Father of our Lord Jesus Christ, who has blessed us with every spiritual blessing in the heavenly places in Christ, just as He chose us in Him before the foundation of the world, that we should be holy and without blame before Him in love, having pre-destined us to adoption as sons by Jesus Christ to Himself, according to the good pleasure of His will.

EPHESIANS 1:3–5

Your Salvation Can't Be Forfeited

Salvation through faith alone cannot be reconciled with the belief that one can forfeit his or her salvation. If I must do or not do something to keep from losing my salvation, salvation would be by faith and works.

I specifically remember the day this particular truth dawned on me. It was as if a light came on. Suddenly, I saw it. I wanted to shout!

That morning introduced me to the true meaning of unconditional love. It was the beginning of my lifelong journey into the mystery of God's truly amazing grace.

~

Thank You for Your amazing grace, dear Lord. I am no longer in bondage. My debt has been paid.

Therefore we also, since we are surrounded by so great a cloud of witnesses, let us lay aside every weight, and the sin which so easily ensnares us, and let us run with endurance the race that is set before us, looking unto Jesus, the author and finisher of our faith, who for the joy that was set before Him endured the cross, despising the shame, and has sat down at the right hand of the throne of God.

HEBREWS 12:1–2

Finally, brethren, whatever things are true, whatever things are noble, whatever things are just, whatever things are pure, whatever things are lovely, whatever things are of good report, if there is any virtue and if there is anything praiseworthy—meditate on these things.

PHILIPPIANS 4:8

How to Change Your Focus

As long as you have an ongoing role in the salvation process, your natural tendency will be to focus on your behavior rather than on Christ. Certainly there is a place for self-examination in the Christian life. But you are certainly not to be the focus of your life.

My observation has been that the more a person focuses on himself, the less he is able to keep his life in order. On the other hand, the more an individual focuses on Christ, the easier it becomes to allow Him to control every area of life.

~

Change my focus, Lord, from me to Thee! Help me lay aside every weight and sin so that I can run the race before me. Let me fix my attention upon You. Settled. Secure.

As many as received Him, to them He gave the right to become children of God, to those who believe in His name.

JOHN 1:12

This is the will of Him who sent Me, that everyone who sees the Son and believes in Him may have everlasting life; and I will raise him up at the last day.

JOHN 6:40

For all have sinned and fall short of the glory of God.

ROMANS 3:23

For the wages of sin is death, but the gift of God is eternal life in Christ Jesus our Lord.

ROMANS 6:23

Your Security Is Eternal

The penalty of your sin was death, physically and spiritually. Faith is the means by which the saving work of Christ is applied to the individual. Salvation comes to you when you place your trust in Christ's death on the cross as the complete payment for sin.

If you have placed your trust in Christ's death on the cross as the payment for your sin, you are an eternal member of the family of God. Acting like God's child didn't get you in. Not acting like one won't get you tossed out. Salvation is forever.

～

I am so glad that my acceptance is not based on performance, Lord. Thank You that salvation is forever. I am a permanent member of Your family.

For you did not receive the spirit of bondage again to fear, but you received the Spirit of adoption by whom we cry out, "Abba, Father." The Spirit Himself bears witness with our spirit that we are children of God.

ROMANS 8:15–16

When the fullness of the time had come, God sent forth His Son, born of a woman, born under the law, to redeem those who were under the law, that we might receive the adoption as sons.

GALATIANS 4:4–5

God Chose You!

The Holy Spirit directed the apostle Paul to use the term *adoption* to describe the process by which God establishes a relationship with a man or woman who trusts Christ as Savior. We are encouraged to think of our heavenly Father in the most intimate way, as a daddy.

God's ultimate goal in salvation was the relationship made available through our adoption. God chose to adopt you as His child before the foundation of the world. Why? For one reason and one reason only: He wanted to.

Thank You for adopting me, Lord. You've changed my nature. You've changed my destiny. I'm family.

To me, who am less than the least of all the saints, this grace was given, that I should preach among the Gentiles the unsearchable riches of Christ, and to make all see what is the fellowship of the mystery, which from the beginning of the ages has been hidden in God who created all things through Jesus Christ.

EPHESIANS 3:8–9

Therefore, just as through one man sin entered the world, and death through sin, and thus death spread to all men, because all sinned.

ROMANS 5:12

The gift is not like that which came through the one who sinned. For the judgment which came from one offense resulted in condemnation, but the free gift which came from many offenses resulted in justification.

ROMANS 5:16

Your Free Gift

You and I are not saved because we have enduring faith. We are saved because at a moment in time we expressed faith in our enduring Lord. Faith is our way of accepting God's gift.

Has there been a time in your life when you accepted God's free gift of salvation? If not, why not settle the issue once and for all right now? God is not looking for a series of promises. He does not want to hear all the things you intend to do for Him. He is more concerned about what you will let Him do for you.

If you are not sure you are saved, why not make sure now? Pray this prayer:

~

God, I know I am a sinner. I believe Christ died in my place at Calvary. I accept His death as the full payment for my sin. I accept Him as my Savior. Amen.

Therefore we make it our aim, whether present or absent, to be well pleasing to Him. For we must all appear before the judgment seat of Christ, that each one may receive the things done in the body, according to what he has done, whether good or bad.

2 CORINTHIANS 5:9–10

And I saw the dead, small and great, standing before God, and books were opened. And another book was opened, which is the Book of Life. And the dead were judged according to their works, by the things which were written in the books. The sea gave up the dead who were in it, and Death and Hades delivered up the dead who were in them. And they were judged, each one according to his works.

REVELATION 20:12–13

Your Works

Does our behavior matter once we are assured of our salvation? You bet it does. Are there any eternal consequences when a believer sins? Absolutely. Will eternity be the same for those who follow Christ faithfully and those who live for themselves? Not a chance.

Our God is a God of justice as well as grace. His grace moved Him to sacrifice His only Son to provide a way for our salvation. But His justice causes Him to take special note of believers who are willing to sacrifice for His Son.

~

Father, someday I will stand before You and give account of my life. I want to hear the words, "Well done."

Let us draw near with a true heart in full assurance of faith, having our hearts sprinkled from an evil conscience and our bodies washed with pure water. Let us hold fast the confession of our hope without wavering, for He who promised is faithful.

HEBREWS 10:22–23

If we walk in the light as He is in the light, we have fellowship with one another, and the blood of Jesus Christ His Son cleanses us from all sin.

1 JOHN 1:7

His Part, Your Part

I can remember a discussion with a missionary who did not believe in once saved, always saved. When I posed the question to him, he said, "Yes, Charles, Christ's blood was adequate, but we have to do our part as well." For him, "our part" included a consistent walk with God—which really boiled down to works.

Christ's blood was adequate to perfect for all time those whom God has sanctified. You need add nothing to it. Your part is to respond to His unconditional love with reverence and obedience while resting in the assurance that your eternity is secure.

~

You've done Your part, Lord. It is finished. It is eternal. Now let me do my part and respond to Your unconditional love with reverence and obedience.

This is a faithful saying:
For if we died with Him,
    We shall also live with Him.
If we endure,
    We shall also reign with Him.
If we deny Him,
    He also will deny us.
If we are faithless,
    He remains faithful;
He cannot deny Himself.

2 TIMOTHY 2:11–13

Your faithfulness endures to all generations;
You established the earth, and it abides.

PSALM 119:90

Through the LORD's mercies we are not consumed,
Because His compassions fail not.
They are new every morning;
Great is Your faithfulness.

LAMENTATIONS 3:22–23

God Remains Faithful to You

Satan wants to destroy your faith. Once that is weakened or gone altogether, you are powerless against him. Your faith is constantly under attack. Some battles you will win; some you will lose. But regardless of the shape your faith is in, your salvation is always intact. For whereas your faith is often tuned in to your changing circumstances, your salvation is anchored in the unchanging nature and grace of God.

God remains faithful, even to the faithless.

~

Heavenly Father, thank You that in the battles of my life, You remain faithful even when I am faithless. Great is Your faithfulness!

Putting the Past Behind You

Do not remember the former things,
Nor consider the things of old.
Behold, I will do a new thing,
Now it shall spring forth;
Shall you not know it?
I will even make a road in the wilderness
And rivers in the desert.

ISAIAH 43:18–19

Whenever you stand praying, if you have anything
against anyone, forgive him, that your Father in heaven
may also forgive you your trespasses.

MARK 11:25

Why You Must Forgive

Forgiveness is something that each of us has had to deal with in one way or another. What might take you just a short time to work through might be a process that takes someone else time, prayer, and godly counsel. But it is a process we cannot ignore, not if we want to be free to become the persons God created us to be. If we refuse to deal with the bitterness and resentments that put us in bondage, we cannot have the fellowship with our Father that we are supposed to have.

~

I realize that time does not heal, dear Lord. Healing comes only as I learn to forgive, but I can't do it in myself. Help me do it in Your strength.

Love your enemies, do good, and lend, hoping for nothing in return; and your reward will be great, and you will be sons of the Most High.

LUKE 6:35

If your enemy is hungry, give him bread to eat;
And if he is thirsty, give him water to drink;
For so you will heap coals of fire on his head,
And the LORD will reward you.

PROVERBS 25:21–22

Bless those who persecute you; bless and do not curse.

ROMANS 12:14

When You Refuse to Forgive

When a person is taken hostage on the international scene, the abductors usually want something. There is always some type of condition, a ransom of some sort.

When individuals refuse to forgive, they are saying the same thing. But instead of holding people hostage until they get their demands, they withhold love, acceptance, respect, service, kindness, patience, or whatever the others value. The message they send is this: "Until I feel you have repaid me for the wrong done to me, you do not have my acceptance."

~

Heavenly Father, take this heavy load of unforgiveness. I am tired of its weight upon my soul. Help me to release my grasp and let it go.

For God so loved the world that He gave His only begotten Son, that whoever believes in Him should not perish but have everlasting life. For God did not send His Son into the world to condemn the world, but that the world through Him might be saved.

JOHN 3:16–17

There is therefore now no condemnation to those who are in Christ Jesus, who do not walk according to the flesh, but according to the Spirit.

ROMANS 8:1

God's Solution for Your Sin

Are there sins from your past that continue to hang over you like a dark cloud? When you pray, does something inside you cause you to doubt that God is going to listen to you because of your past? Do you feel that your potential for the kingdom of God has been destroyed because of your past disobedience? If you answered yes to any of these questions, you have not yet come to grips with God's solution to your sin.

Christ is God's solution for dealing with sin. Only through Christ can you find forgiveness. Sin is sin; lost is lost; paid is paid; forgiven is forgiven.

~

Dear Lord, thank You for saving me from the penalty and power of sin. Help me walk in the reality of Your solution for my sin. Release me from my past.

I write to you, little children,
Because your sins are forgiven you for His name's sake.

1 JOHN 2:12

Look on my affliction and my pain,
And forgive all my sins.

PSALM 25:18

Bless the LORD, O my soul;
And all that is within me,
    bless His holy name!
Bless the LORD, O my soul,
And forget not all His benefits:
Who forgives all your iniquities,
Who heals all your diseases.

PSALM 103:1–3

You Are Forgiven

God wants us to live with perfect assurance that we are completely forgiven. If we have placed our trust in God's system of forgiveness, that means there is no difference between the sins we have committed, are committing, and will commit. None! Remember, forgiven is forgiven.

In one sense, living in a state of forgiveness can be compared to having a checking account with unlimited funds available. It would be impossible for us to incur debts as long as we write checks and continue to draw on our account.

~

It's settled, Lord, once and for all—my past, present, and future sins are forgiven. Thank You for the unlimited resources of my spiritual account upon which I may freely draw.

Moreover the law entered that the offense might abound. But where sin abounded, grace abounded much more, so that as sin reigned in death, even so grace might reign through righteousness to eternal life through Jesus Christ our Lord.

ROMANS 5:20–21

The grace of God that brings salvation has appeared to all men.

TITUS 2:11

Your Past Is a Memorial

You may be thinking, *Every time I pray I think about the things I have done, and I feel alienated from God. I cannot pray with any confidence or assurance.*

First, you must settle in your mind once and for all that your sins are forgiven; that God is in no way holding them against you; that from His perspective, they are no longer obstacles to fellowship.

Second, you must begin to view your past failures as reminders of God's grace. Your past sins should become memorials to the grace of God in your life.

~

I marvel, Lord, that You can take my past and use it for Your glory. Help me view every sin, each failure, and every time I stumbled and fell as memorials to Your work of grace in my life.

Brethren, I do not count myself to have apprehended; but one thing I do, forgetting those things which are behind and reaching forward to those things which are ahead, I press toward the goal for the prize of the upward call of God in Christ Jesus.

PHILIPPIANS 3:13–14

If we say that we have no sin, we deceive ourselves, and the truth is not in us. If we confess our sins, He is faithful and just to forgive us our sins and to cleanse us from all unrighteousness.

1 JOHN 1:8–9

How to Forgive Yourself

How do you forgive yourself? Regardless of how long you have been in bondage, you can be free if you follow four biblical steps:

Step 1: Recognize the problem.
Step 2: Repent of sin.
Step 3: Reaffirm trust.
Step 4: Confess freedom and choose to receive it.

If you follow these steps, not only will you be set free, but the healing process will be initiated.

~

Father, I reaffirm my trust and faith in the Word of God that my transgressions are removed. I here and now forgive myself because You have already forgiven me.

Then Peter came to Him and said, "Lord, how often shall my brother sin against me, and I forgive him? Up to seven times?" Jesus said to him, "I do not say to you, up to seven times, but up to seventy times seven."

MATTHEW 18:21–22

And forgive us our debts,
As we forgive our debtors. . . .
For if you forgive men their trespasses, your heavenly Father will also forgive you. But if you do not forgive men their trespasses, neither will your Father forgive your trespasses.

MATTHEW 6:12, 14–15

You Can Forgive Others

Forgiveness is an act of the will that involves five steps:

1. Remember that you have been forgiven.
2. Forgive the debt.
3. Accept others.
4. View others as tools of growth.
5. Make reconciliation.

After completing these five steps in forgiveness, pray this simple prayer:

~

Lord, I forgive (name) *for* (name the specifics). *I do this in Your power. I do it as an act of my will. I forgive the debt because You forgave my debt.*

Take heed to yourselves. If your brother sins against you, rebuke him; and if he repents, forgive him.

LUKE 17:3

Having been set free from sin, you became slaves of righteousness.

ROMANS 6:18

Bearing with one another, and forgiving one another, if anyone has a complaint against another; even as Christ forgave you, so you also must do.

COLOSSIANS 3:13

Be kind to one another, tenderhearted, forgiving one another, even as God in Christ forgave you.

EPHESIANS 4:32

How Long Will You Remain Imprisoned?

Forgiveness is liberating, but it is also sometimes painful. It is liberating because we are freed from the heavy load of guilt, bitterness, and anger we have harbored within. It is painful because it is difficult to have to face ourselves, God, and others with our failures.

Are you still unable to forgive someone who hurt you deeply and you still bear the scars? How long will you remain a prisoner to your unforgiving spirit? You have within you the power to forgive, to be healed, and to be set free to live your life to the fullest.

~

Lord, You have spoken words of truth. I accept Your message. I am free to forgive and be forgiven.

WINNING THE WAR WITHIN YOU

For we do not wrestle against flesh and blood, but against principalities, against powers, against the rulers of the darkness of this age, against spiritual hosts of wickedness in the heavenly places.

EPHESIANS 6:12

Now then, we are ambassadors for Christ, as though God were pleading through us: we implore you on Christ's behalf, be reconciled to God.

2 CORINTHIANS 5:20

You therefore must endure hardship as a good soldier of Jesus Christ. No one engaged in warfare entangles himself with the affairs of this life, that he may please him who enlisted him as a soldier.

2 TIMOTHY 2:3–4

You Are an Ambassador

When you hear the term *temptation*, what flashes into your mind?

All of our struggles are spiritual in nature. Each one is a part of an ongoing struggle between the kingdom of God and the kingdom of Satan.

When I am being tempted with the little things that pop up every day, I tend to think that it is just my little problem and that no one else will be affected. I forget that I am an ambassador for Christ and that every victory—no matter how small—is a sign to the "spiritual forces" that Jesus is alive and working.

~

Thank You for victory, Lord, over every temptation, each trial and struggle. Let me view each battle as a spiritual conflict. Help me be a good ambassador.

I acknowledged my sin to You,

And my iniquity I have not hidden.

I said, "I will confess my transgressions to the LORD,"

And You forgave the iniquity of my sin.

PSALM 32:5

For I will declare my iniquity;

I will be in anguish over my sin.

PSALM 38:18

Wash me thoroughly from my iniquity,

And cleanse me from my sin.

For I acknowledge my transgressions,

And my sin is always before me.

Against You, You only, have I sinned,

And done this evil in Your sight—

That You may be found just when You speak,

And blameless when You judge.

PSALM 51:2–4

Dealing with Your Besetting Sin

We don't like to take complete responsibility for our temptations. Yet this tendency keeps many of us from dealing successfully with the besetting sins in our lives.

Blaming someone or something else for your particular weaknesses and temptations appears to take the responsibility off your shoulders. But by mentally removing yourself from a position of responsibility, you also remove yourself from a position wherein you could correct the situation. Until you are willing to take responsibility for your failures, you will be unwilling and therefore unable to do anything about them.

~

Help me take responsibility for my failures, heavenly Father. Cleanse me from secret faults. Search me, purify me, then use me for Your glory.

All things are lawful for me, but all things are not help-
ful. All things are lawful for me, but I will not be
brought under the power of any.

1 Corinthians 6:12

I beseech you therefore, brethren, by the mercies of God,
that you present your bodies a living sacrifice, holy,
acceptable to God, which is your reasonable service.
And do not be conformed to this world, but be trans-
formed by the renewing of your mind, that you may
prove what is that good and acceptable and perfect will
of God.

Romans 12:1–2

Putting Bad Habits Behind You

Many people blame their personality for their inability to deal successfully with particular temptations. They say, "That's just the way I am," or "I've always been this way." Often accompanying this way of thinking is a plea to "accept me the way I am."

Do you expect people to accept and adjust to your peculiarities? Have you been using your personality as an excuse for the way you are rather than trying to change? If you have, it is time to quit making excuses and begin making progress. To do otherwise is to rob yourself and others of the joy that comes with the freedom of putting bad habits behind you.

~

Father, I've used a lot of excuses for my behavior. I acknowledge my sin and ask Your forgiveness. Help me be not what I was or even what I am, but what You want me to be.

For since the creation of the world His invisible attributes are clearly seen, being understood by the things that are made, even His eternal power and Godhead, so that they are without excuse.

ROMANS 1:20

Behold, I give you the authority to trample on serpents and scorpions, and over all the power of the enemy, and nothing shall by any means hurt you.

LUKE 10:19

Exhort one another daily, while it is called "Today," lest any of you be hardened through the deceitfulness of sin.

HEBREWS 3:13

You Are Responsible

Have you fallen into the habit of making excuses for the recurring sins in your life? Have you found a person or a group of people on whom you can blame your failures?

The first step in overcoming temptation is to stop deceiving yourself into thinking that someone or something else is responsible for your actions. God didn't accept Adam's and Eve's attempts to shift the blame. He doesn't accept yours, either. Who is to blame for your failure to deal successfully with temptation? You are. To face up to this fact is to take a giant step toward overcoming temptation.

~

Heavenly Father, there are no excuses for my failures. No reasons that will suffice. No justifications. But there is reconciliation—and I claim that now through Jesus Christ.

Now if God so clothes the grass of the field, which today is, and tomorrow is thrown into the oven, will He not much more clothe you, O you of little faith? Therefore do not worry, saying, "What shall we eat?" or "What shall we drink?" or "What shall we wear?" For after all these things the Gentiles seek. For your heavenly Father knows that you need all these things. But seek first the kingdom of God and His righteousness, and all these things shall be added to you.

MATTHEW 6:30–33

What Do You Really Need?

God does not intend for you to live a life full of frustration and anxiety. On the contrary, Satan is the one who wants your life to be filled with anxiety. That is why he is always so quick to offer a substitute for God's best. He knows his offer will not satisfy. He also knows that if he can get you hooked on his alternative, many times you will completely miss God's best.

God does not promise to meet your need immediately. What He promises is the peace of God, that is, the inner strength to endure until your desires and needs are fulfilled.

~

What I think I need and what I really need are two different things, Lord. Help me recognize the difference and trust You for my true needs. Make me willing to wait.

For we do not have a High Priest who cannot sympathize with our weaknesses, but was in all points tempted as we are, yet without sin.

HEBREWS 4:15

When you pass through the waters, I will be with you;
And through the rivers, they shall not overflow you.
When you walk through the fire, you shall not be
    burned,
Nor shall the flame scorch you.

ISAIAH 43:2

For in that He Himself has suffered, being tempted, He is able to aid those who are tempted.

HEBREWS 2:18

God Limits Your Temptations

God has put limitations on our temptations. This assures us of three things:

First, we will never be tempted more than we can bear—never!

Second, God is involved in our struggle against temptation.

Third, God is faithful; He can be trusted.

Many people live or work in situations where they are constantly being tempted to sin. Oftentimes there is no place or opportunity for them to run. God is faithful even in those situations. He will always provide a way out.

~

Thank You, dear Lord, that You have set the limits to my temptation. I will never be tempted above what I can bear! I am glad You are involved in my struggles. Thank You for being the referee instead of only a spectator.

"No weapon formed against you shall prosper,
And every tongue which rises against you in judgment
You shall condemn.
This is the heritage of the servants of the LORD,
And their righteousness is from Me,"
Says the LORD.

ISAIAH 54:17

Therefore we do not lose heart. Even though our outward man is perishing, yet the inward man is being renewed day by day. For our light affliction, which is but for a moment, is working for us a far more exceeding and eternal weight of glory.

2 CORINTHIANS 4:16–17

Seeing Your Temptations as God Sees Them

God does not want us to be ignorant about temptation. He wants us to know the truth. For example, running is not always the best way to overcome temptation. There is a time to run and a time to stand.

Until you begin to see your temptations the way God sees them, you will feel a weight of responsibility God never intended for you to feel; your expectation level will remain totally unrealistic. Consequently, you will become discouraged and unmotivated. God wants you to be free, and that freedom comes through knowing the truth.

~

Help me see my temptations as You see them, dear Lord. Give me a new perspective. Let me know when to run and when to stand firm while You accomplish Your purposes.

Sin shall not have dominion over you, for you are not under law but under grace.

ROMANS 6:14

Therefore, brethren, we are debtors—not to the flesh, to live according to the flesh. For if you live according to the flesh you will die; but if by the Spirit you put to death the deeds of the body, you will live.

ROMANS 8:12–13

Be strong in the Lord and in the power of His might.

EPHESIANS 6:10

Your Power Potential

God provides the power to overcome temptation.

First, power determines potential.

Second, power must be harnessed and applied toward a specific goal before it serves any purpose.

Third, power, when harnessed and focused, can greatly extend the potential of the one in whose hands the power rests.

Believers have the potential to say no to the devil, no to the flesh, and no to sin.

~

Thank You for power, Lord, over all the power of the enemy! Help me harness Your power and focus it to maximize my spiritual potential. I begin right now by saying no to Satan, no to the flesh, and no to sin!

Put on the whole armor of God, that you may be able to stand against the wiles of the devil. For we do not wrestle against flesh and blood, but against principalities, against powers, against the rulers of the darkness of this age, against spiritual hosts of wickedness in the heavenly places. Therefore take up the whole armor of God, that you may be able to withstand in the evil day, and having done all, to stand. Stand therefore, having girded your waist with truth, having put on the breastplate of righteousness, and having shod your feet with the preparation of the gospel of peace; above all, taking the shield of faith with which you will be able to quench all the fiery darts of the wicked one. And take the helmet of salvation, and the sword of the Spirit, which is the word of God.

EPHESIANS 6:11–17

54

Don't Forget Your Armor

I have made a habit of putting on the armor of God every morning before I get out of bed. Remember, this is spiritual armor. Therefore, it must be put on by faith. Paul understood that spiritual warfare was somewhat of a difficult concept to grasp. So he gave us an illustration through his description of the Roman soldier. Using that mental image as a guide, we can properly prepare ourselves for the battle. But it is done by faith, not by sight.

~

I put on the helmet of salvation and bind discouragement and depression. I put on the breastplate of righteousness and bind unrighteousness. I put on the girdle of truth and bind deception. I put on shoes to walk in Your ways, Father, and I take the sword of the Spirit of Your Word in my hands to conquer the enemy.

For the word of God is living and powerful, and sharper than any two-edged sword, piercing even to the division of soul and spirit, and of joints and marrow, and is a discerner of the thoughts and intents of the heart.

Hebrews 4:12

Your word I have hidden in my heart,
That I might not sin against You.

Psalm 119:11

Blessed are those who keep His testimonies,
Who seek Him with the whole heart!
They also do no iniquity;
They walk in His ways.

Psalm 119:2–3

How can a young man cleanse his way?
By taking heed according to Your word.

Psalm 119:9

Your Spiritual Arsenal

There are four reasons that a well-chosen passage or verse of Scripture is so effective against temptation.

First of all, God's Word exposes the sinfulness of whatever you are being tempted to do. Second, the Scripture provides you with a divine perspective on the temptation you are facing as well as your relationship to it. Third, the Scripture gives you something godly to focus your thoughts on. Fourth, you are expressing faith when you turn your attention to His Word.

To effectively combat the onslaughts of the enemy, you need an arsenal of verses on the tip of your tongue.

~

Lord, Your Word is my protection. I want to hide it in my heart so that in the heat of battle I can draw upon its unlimited resources.

Healing

your

Damaged

Emotions

He Himself has said, "I will never leave you nor forsake you."

HEBREWS 13:5

Lo, I am with you always, even to the end of the age.

MATTHEW 28:20

If I take the wings of the morning,
And dwell in the uttermost parts of the sea,
Even there Your hand shall lead me,
And Your right hand shall hold me.

PSALM 139:9–10

You Are Never Alone

You simply cannot be alone once you have the Spirit of God dwelling in you. You can experience a tormenting feeling of emptiness, fear, or desperation. You can feel alone even though you are not alone. These feelings are subject to what you do about them. You can let your feelings drive you away from the Lord—and experience less intimacy with Him. Or you can let these feelings drive you toward the Lord and to an even greater intimacy.

The Lord invites you to cling to Him. He says to you, "Lean on Me."

~

Lord, free me from loneliness. Be my total and complete satisfaction. Fill the void in my life. I am tired of feeling alone.

My God shall supply all your need according to His riches in glory by Christ Jesus.

PHILIPPIANS 4:19

God has not given us a spirit of fear, but of power and of love and of a sound mind.

2 TIMOTHY 1:7

I have been young, and now am old;
Yet I have not seen the righteous forsaken,
Nor his descendants begging bread.

PSALM 37:25

Are You Trusting God?

If you are struggling with fear and worry, there are four questions you are wise to ask yourself on a daily basis:

1. Am I trusting God today to provide my daily needs?
2. Am I trusting God to be my security today?
3. Am I willing to risk some of what I have today because I am trusting God to meet my needs tomorrow?
4. Am I trusting You today, Lord, to show me Your way?

~

Father, You promised to meet all my needs. You can make me adequate for all things and every circumstance. Take my fears and anxieties. I'm trusting You to be in control.

Now, therefore, you are no longer strangers and foreigners, but fellow citizens with the saints and members of the household of God.

EPHESIANS 2:19

In Him also we have obtained an inheritance, being predestined according to the purpose of Him who works all things according to the counsel of His will, that we who first trusted in Christ should be to the praise of His glory.

EPHESIANS 1:11–12

It's Time to Change Your Tape

When people find themselves in an abusive situation, they frequently begin to play what I call the victim tape. They hear all the old messages. For example: "You can't do it," "You aren't worthy of it," "You'll never be able to handle it," "You aren't good enough," and "You deserve what you're getting."

We need to take action to change the messages on the victim tape. Then we must put a new message on the tape: "The truth of the matter is, I am a joint heir in Christ Jesus of all God's benefits."

~

Stop the tape—and then help me change it, Lord. I am tired of listening to reruns. Write Your new message on the recorder of my innermost being.

I, even I, am He who blots out your transgressions for
   My own sake;
And I will not remember your sins.
   ISAIAH 43:25

As far as the east is from the west,
So far has He removed our transgressions from us.
   PSALM 103:12

Hide Your face from my sins,
And blot out all my iniquities.
   PSALM 51:9

How God Handles Your Failures

God has the ability to forgive. He has the ability to turn your failures into triumphs. He is able to figure out a place that's just right for your particular talents and gifts. And furthermore, He desires to put you to use in His kingdom.

It is not the Lord who reminds you of past sins that you have already confessed to Him. He won't bring to your remembrance something He has forgotten! Such haunting memories are inspired from the enemy of your soul, the devil. When you are confronted with images or memories of sins you have already confessed to God, it's time to say . . .

~

I refuse to accept these thoughts. God has already forgiven me of my past sins. I'm letting this thought go right on by. Devil, you'll have no hold on my mind!

The LORD is my light and my salvation;
Whom shall I fear?
The LORD is the strength of my life;
Of whom shall I be afraid?

PSALM 27:1

God is our refuge and strength,
A very present help in trouble.

PSALM 46:1

Not that we are sufficient of ourselves to think of anything as being from ourselves, but our sufficiency is from God.

2 CORINTHIANS 3:5

When You Are Feeling Inadequate

If you are in a position where you know that you cannot do something in and of your own strength, and that unless you completely trust God to do the work in you and through you, you will fail, then you are in the best possible position for the task to be accomplished. God knew before He asked you to do something that you couldn't do it by yourself. Ask the Lord to show you the first step that you need to take toward the goal. Do what He shows you to do with all your strength, might, and talent. And then look for the second step that He leads you to take.

~

I cannot do this, God, but You can. I'm willing to do whatever You tell me to do, but You'll have to provide the energy, the ideas, the resources, and the talent in order for this to get done.

Come to Me, all you who labor and are heavy laden,
and I will give you rest.

MATTHEW 11:28

Cast your burden on the LORD,
And He shall sustain you;
He shall never permit the righteous to be moved.

PSALM 55:22

Casting all your care upon Him, for He cares for you.

1 PETER 5:7

When You Are Feeling Burned Out

W hen you are feeling burned out . . .

- Put yourself into a position to rest. Take a long enough break for your body to mend, your mind to clear, and your heart to heal.
- Ask the Lord to show you how to trust Him more.
- Admit to the Lord that you are responsible for your burnout tendencies. Ask the Lord to show you what to do about the inner pain and emotional baggage that may be driving you to strive relentlessly for approval and perfection.

~

Lord, take the inner pain and the driving force within me causing restlessness and frustration. I release the responsibilities of my life to You. Show me how to lighten my load.

Peace I leave with you, My peace I give to you; not as the world gives do I give to you. Let not your heart be troubled, neither let it be afraid.

JOHN 14:27

Not that I speak in regard to need, for I have learned in whatever state I am, to be content.

PHILIPPIANS 4:11

Godliness with contentment is great gain.

1 TIMOTHY 6:6

You Can Find Contentment

The world is always going to have irritants in it. Unwise decisions and sinful situations abound. They have nothing, however, to do with the state of your inner soul. You can be content on the inside, no matter what kinds and amounts of sin or error swirl around you.

The answer to frustration and restlessness comes as you trust God. You trust Him to be your shelter, your safety from life's storms and turmoil. You trust Him to be your wisdom against error and false starts. You trust Him to be your peace.

~

Thank You, heavenly Father, that You are my shelter. You provide wisdom to protect me from error and safety from life's storms. Let me find true contentment in You.

O GOD the Lord, the strength of my salvation,
You have covered my head in the day of battle.
    PSALM 140:7

He calms the storm,
So that its waves are still.
    PSALM 107:29

For You have been a strength to the poor,
A strength to the needy in his distress,
A refuge from the storm,
A shade from the heat;
For the blast of the terrible ones is as a storm against
    the wall.
    ISAIAH 25:4

Bind Yourself to the Mast

In centuries past, sailors and even captains of ships would bind themselves to the ship's mast to keep from being swept overboard by giant waves that threatened to capsize the vessel. In that manner, they'd ride out the storm, trusting in God to calm the winds and waves.

When the storms rage against us—and we find ourselves sailing in waters where we know the Lord has led us—we must do likewise. We must bind ourselves to the mast of the Lord Jesus and hold tight, trust in God to rebuke the storm that is raging against us, and, at the same time, preserve our lives and keep us strong in our faith.

~

I'm experiencing a tempest, God. The wind is howling, and the billows are raging. Right now, I am binding myself to the mast of the Lord Jesus. Let me cling fast until this storm has passed.

Who shall separate us from the love of Christ? Shall tribulation, or distress, or persecution, or famine, or nakedness, or peril, or sword? . . . Yet in all these things we are more than conquerors through Him who loved us. For I am persuaded that neither death nor life, nor angels nor principalities nor powers, nor things present nor things to come, nor height nor depth, nor any other created thing, shall be able to separate us from the love of God which is in Christ Jesus our Lord.

ROMANS 8:35, 37–39

Crisis Is Your Launching Pad

It is vital for us to realize that a continuing or lingering emotional pain is a signal to us from the Lord. It is a message that He wants to do something in our lives—that He isn't content for us to carry that weight in our hearts any longer. Emotional pain can, and must, be seen as an initiative from God that will draw us to Him so that He may heal us.

Failures and hurts can be a key to discovering who God wants you to be. Trauma, grief, and crisis can be the launching pads that move you from one level of personal spiritual growth to another. The challenge you face is in how you choose to respond to those times.

~

Let me see my crisis as You see it, Lord—a launching pad to move me to a higher level in You. Help me trust You in difficult circumstances, knowing You are working all things together for my good.

Behold, I have refined you, but not as silver;
I have tested you in the furnace of affliction.

ISAIAH 48:10

You did not choose Me, but I chose you and appointed
you that you should go and bear fruit, and that your
fruit should remain, that whatever you ask the Father in
My name He may give you.

JOHN 15:16

Listen, my beloved brethren: Has God not chosen the
poor of this world to be rich in faith and heirs of the
kingdom which He promised to those who love Him?

JAMES 2:5

God Thinks You're Fantastic!

Your self-esteem must be based on God's opinion, not someone else's opinion or even your opinion. Your self-esteem is to be based on what God thinks. And God thinks you are fantastic!

The Lord doesn't ask us to be perfect. But He does call us to follow His perfect will. The Lord doesn't ask us to succeed in the eyes of others. He does ask us to seek to live the life that is acceptable to Him—a life of sacrifice, giving, and complete and utter reliance upon the Lord Jesus Christ. Jesus never said, "Do your best." He said, "Follow Me."

~

Lord, true success is determined by what You think of me. Your Word to me this day is simply to follow. I'm ready—just show me the way.

Advancing through your Adversities

We are hard pressed on every side, yet not crushed; we are perplexed, but not in despair; persecuted, but not forsaken; struck down, but not destroyed—always carrying about in the body the dying of the Lord Jesus, that the life of Jesus also may be manifested in our body.

2 CORINTHIANS 4:8–10

You have caused men to ride over our heads;
We went through fire and through water;
But You brought us out to rich fulfillment.

PSALM 66:12

There's Something Exciting in Store for You

If you are facing adversity in your life, God may be trying to get your attention. He may be trying to draw your attention to a specific sin. God may know that you are on the verge of making a major mistake in your life; perhaps He wants to intensify His relationship with you during this time of decision making. Whatever your circumstances may be, rest assured that God does not do things without a purpose. If He has allowed adversity to enter your world, He has something exciting in store for you!

~

Dear Lord, I know You have purpose in my problems. Change my focus from reasons to response, from temporal to eternal, from human to divine.

He heals the brokenhearted
And binds up their wounds.

PSALM 147:3

O LORD my God, I cried out to You,
And You healed me.

PSALM 30:2

He sent His word and healed them,
And delivered them from their destructions.

PSALM 107:20

The Deeper Your Hurt, the Greater His Comfort

When I was a little boy, I sustained my share of scraped knees and stubbed toes. Iodine has an orange-colored tint that even looks as though it would sting—which it did. After the tiny applicator was rubbed on my wound and I was still loudly protesting, my mother did a wonderful thing. She would gently blow on the stinging spot. My cries lessened as she soothed my body and, most of all, my heart.

That is perhaps one of the sweetest pictures to me of the God of all comfort. He, by the Holy Spirit, breathes comfort upon the scrapes and wounds of life. The deeper the hurt, the more gentle the blowing.

~

Lord, I hurt. Blow gently upon my wounds by the breath of Your Holy Spirit. Bind up the scrapes and hurts of my life. Pour in Your healing oil.

In the day when I cried out, You answered me,
And made me bold with strength in my soul.

PSALM 138:3

We know that all things work together for good to those who love God, to those who are the called according to His purpose. For whom He foreknew, He also predestined to be conformed to the image of His Son, that He might be the firstborn among many brethren.

ROMANS 8:28–29

Your Response to Adversity

Have you been so hung up on trying to figure out why adversity has come your way that perhaps you have missed God? Has the adversity in your life strengthened your faith, or has it weakened your faith? Adversity is a reality that none of us can avoid. Therefore, it is in your best interest to begin responding in such a way that the negative can be used to accomplish the will of God in your life. And as you begin responding correctly, perhaps you will begin to understand why.

~

Forgive me, Lord, for the way I respond in trouble. Help me realize You create beauty from ashes, joy from mourning, life from death. Accomplish Your purposes in my problems.

My brethren, count it all joy when you fall into various trials, knowing that the testing of your faith produces patience. But let patience have its perfect work, that you may be perfect and complete, lacking nothing.

JAMES 1:2–4

The LORD also will be a refuge for the oppressed,
A refuge in times of trouble.
And those who know Your name will put their trust
   in You;
For You, LORD, have not forsaken those who seek You.

PSALM 9:9–10

Don't Rob Yourself

James is very clear as to why we are to be joyous in the midst of adversity. He states it, however, in the form of an assumption rather than a reason. James assumes that his readers are so committed to spiritual growth that when they understand that trials lead to more spiritual growth, they will rejoice because of the end result—growth! The "testing" of our faith produces endurance. Endurance is a maturing factor.

By resisting adversity, we rob ourselves of the work God desires to do in our lives. We put off the very thing God sent the adversity into our lives to accomplish.

~

I can't honestly say I have been counting it joy to suffer. Forgive me, dear Lord. Help me embrace the difficult times with anticipation of what You will do in my life.

Behold, happy is the man whom God corrects;
Therefore do not despise the chastening of the
Almighty.
For He bruises, but He binds up;
He wounds, but His hands make whole.
He shall deliver you in six troubles,
Yes, in seven no evil shall touch you.
JOB 5:17–19

You, who have shown me great and severe troubles,
Shall revive me again,
And bring me up again from the depths of the earth.
PSALM 71:20

View Your Adversity from God's Perspective

For a long time I had trouble accepting the connection between adversity and growth. My problem, when I got right down to it, was faith. It was hard for me to accept that God is so intent on bringing us to maturity that He is willing to let us suffer. In His economy, adversity is a small price to pay for the benefits of spiritual growth. The issue was whether or not I was going to take God at His word and begin viewing adversity from that perspective.

I think my wavering back and forth is exactly what James was talking about when he said we must ask "in faith." That is, when God reveals the answer, we must accept it.

~

Open my eyes, Lord, so that I can see my situation from Your perspective. I realize adversity is a small price to pay for the benefits of spiritual maturity. Help me to accept Your word.

We have this treasure in earthen vessels, that the excellence of the power may be of God and not of us.

2 CORINTHIANS 4:7

Therefore I take pleasure in infirmities, in reproaches, in needs, in persecutions, in distresses, for Christ's sake. For when I am weak, then I am strong.

2 CORINTHIANS 12:10

God has chosen the foolish things of the world to put to shame the wise, and God has chosen the weak things of the world to put to shame the things which are mighty; and the base things of the world and the things which are despised God has chosen, and the things which are not, to bring to nothing the things that are, that no flesh should glory in His presence.

1 CORINTHIANS 1:27–29

God Is Looking for Someone Like You

God wants people through whom He can show His mighty power, people who know their weaknesses and are willing to allow Him to control and direct their lives. God is looking for men and women who are willing to take on challenges too difficult for them to handle, trusting Him to carry the load. He wants people who understand from experience what Paul meant when he wrote, "My [God's] grace is sufficient for you"—believers who grow accustomed to weakness, but who draw daily upon the sufficiency and power of Christ.

~

I emphasize strength, dear Lord, but You focus on my weaknesses. Make me strong in weakness as You infuse me with Your power. Help me trade my insufficiency for Your sufficiency.

That the genuineness of your faith, being much more precious than gold that perishes, though it is tested by fire, may be found to praise, honor, and glory at the revelation of Jesus Christ.

1 PETER 1:7

That the sharing of your faith may become effective by the acknowledgment of every good thing which is in you in Christ Jesus.

PHILEMON 6

Now faith is the substance of things hoped for, the evidence of things not seen.

HEBREWS 11:1

Let God Increase Your Faith

You may have heard it said that a person does not really know who his friends are until the bottom drops out. The ultimate measure of friends is not where they stand in times of comfort and convenience, but where they stand in times of challenge and controversy. That being the case, apart from adversity of some kind, we would never know who our faithful friends really are.

In the same way, we will never know in a personal way the faithfulness of Christ apart from adversity. One of the primary reasons God allows us to face adversity is so that He can demonstrate His faithfulness and in turn increase our faith.

~

Father, thank You for being my Friend when all others forsake me. I'm glad my circumstances don't have to change for You to be there. Rather, You are right there in the midst of my problems to change the circumstances.

That I may know Him and the power of His resurrection, and the fellowship of His sufferings, being conformed to His death.

PHILIPPIANS 3:10

I have heard of You by the hearing of the ear,
But now my eye sees You.

JOB 42:5

Before I was afflicted I went astray,
But now I keep Your word. . . .
It is good for me that I have been afflicted,
That I may learn Your statutes. . . .
I know, O LORD, that Your judgments are right,
And that in faithfulness You have afflicted me.

PSALM 119:67, 71, 75

Your Potential for Intimacy

Through the death of Christ, God has opened the way for us to have direct access to Him. He went to great lengths to clear the way so that nothing stands between Him and His children. There is potential now for intimacy between us and our Creator.

God is in the process of engineering circumstances through which He can reveal Himself to each of us. And both history and our personal testimonies bear witness to the fact that it is in times of adversity that we come to a greater realization of God's incredible faithfulness to us.

~

Maximize my potential for intimacy, O God. Engineer my circumstances to reveal Yourself to me. I don't just want to know about You; I want to know You.

He said to me, "My grace is sufficient for you, for My strength is made perfect in weakness." Therefore most gladly I will rather boast in my infirmities, that the power of Christ may rest upon me.

2 CORINTHIANS 12:9

He gives more grace. Therefore He says:
"God resists the proud,
But gives grace to the humble."

JAMES 4:6

By the grace of God I am what I am, and His grace toward me was not in vain; but I labored more abundantly than they all, yet not I, but the grace of God which was with me.

1 CORINTHIANS 15:10

His Grace Is Sufficient for You

Perhaps God has chosen to leave your circumstances the way they are. You may never feel any better. Your spouse may never return. You may never recover financially to the economic level you had previously attained. But God is no less faithful, for He will provide you with mercy and grace in time of need.

The Lord did not say to Paul, "My grace will be sufficient for you," or "My grace has been sufficient for you." He said, "My grace is sufficient." That's in the present tense; that means right now. And so it can be in your experience if you will choose to trust Him.

~

Father, help me accept the fact that You may not change my circumstances, but You can change me. Your grace is sufficient for my need. If You choose not to deliver me, then sustain me in the midst of trouble.

Blessed be the God and Father of our Lord Jesus Christ, the Father of mercies and God of all comfort, who comforts us in all our tribulation, that we may be able to comfort those who are in any trouble, with the comfort with which we ourselves are comforted by God.

2 CORINTHIANS 1:3–4

Now if we are afflicted, it is for your consolation and salvation, which is effective for enduring the same sufferings which we also suffer. Or if we are comforted, it is for your consolation and salvation.

2 CORINTHIANS 1:6

Don't Miss Your Ministry

God is in the process of making you a comforter. He is structuring your experience in such a way as to prepare you for a ministry in someone else's life.

The individuals who have allowed (or are allowing) God to walk with them through trials are the ones prepared to comfort others. These people have faced their hurts squarely, drawn on the power of Christ within them, and then put it all in perspective and moved on. These men and women are ready to comfort others.

Are you aiding the process by drawing on His divine power?

~

Whatever it takes, Lord—I don't want to miss my ministry. Structure my experiences so that I will be equipped to fulfill Your purposes. Help me work with the process, not against it. Comfort me that I might comfort others.

LIVING YOUR LIFE IN THE SPIRIT

Being assembled together with them, He commanded them not to depart from Jerusalem, but to wait for the Promise of the Father, "which," He said, "you have heard from Me; for John truly baptized with water, but you shall be baptized with the Holy Spirit not many days from now. . . . But you shall receive power when the Holy Spirit has come upon you; and you shall be witnesses to Me in Jerusalem, and in all Judea and Samaria, and to the end of the earth."

ACTS 1:4–5, 8

You Can't Do It Alone!

The Christian life is not simply difficult. It is not something that gets easier with time. It is not something you grow into. It's impossible. You can't live it. I can't live it. God doesn't expect us to live it. He knows it's impossible. Jesus knew it was impossible. It is time that we come to grips with this liberating truth—it is impossible.

I meet people all the time who say something to the effect of, "I tried to live the Christian life, but it doesn't work." I've got some good news. Christianity is not the problem. More than likely, the problem is that you have been trying to live it apart from the help of the Holy Spirit.

~

I can't grow into it. I can't make it happen. Father, I can't live the Christian life apart from Your Holy Spirit. Liberate me from self-effort.

And I will pray the Father, and He will give you another Helper, that He may abide with you forever—the Spirit of truth, whom the world cannot receive, because it neither sees Him nor knows Him; but you know Him, for He dwells with you and will be in you.

JOHN 14:16–17

Nevertheless I tell you the truth. It is to your advantage that I go away; for if I do not go away, the Helper will not come to you; but if I depart, I will send Him to you.

JOHN 16:7

You Need the Helper

If there ever was a group of people who should have been able to live a consistent Christian life by just doing their best, it was the apostles. They had been trained by the Master, after all. Yet in their last encounter with the Savior, He let them know that they were still missing something. They needed the Holy Spirit.

If eleven men who had walked and talked with Jesus needed the Holy Spirit, how much more do we need Him? Apart from the Helper, life is reduced to doing the best we can. And I don't know about you, but for me that's not very good.

~

I need the Helper, dear Lord. Be my partner, Holy Spirit. Walk with me each day. Talk with me. Guide each step, every word and deed.

Do you not know that you are the temple of God and that the Spirit of God dwells in you?

1 CORINTHIANS 3:16

When He had said this, He breathed on them, and said to them, "Receive the Holy Spirit."

JOHN 20:22

For by one Spirit we were all baptized into one body— whether Jews or Greeks, whether slaves or free—and have all been made to drink into one Spirit.

1 CORINTHIANS 12:13

Get Acquainted with the Spirit

The Holy Spirit knows the thoughts of God. And the Holy Spirit imparts knowledge to believers. The Holy Spirit makes decisions. He has a mind and will of His own. To tap into the Holy Spirit is not to enhance one's ability to carry out one's will. Oh, no! On the contrary, the power of the Holy Spirit is available only to those whose intention is to carry out His will.

The Spirit-filled life is characterized by keeping in step with the Holy Spirit. It will be much easier to follow Him if you know Him, if you have a relationship with Him, and if you can recognize His fingerprint in the daily affairs of your life.

~

Holy Spirit, You know God's thoughts. You know His will. You are the essence of His power. I need to know His thoughts and His will and be endued with power. That is why I need You.

For the fruit of the Spirit is in all goodness, righteousness, and truth.

EPHESIANS 5:9

For this reason we also thank God without ceasing, because when you received the word of God which you heard from us, you welcomed it not as the word of men, but as it is in truth, the word of God, which also effectively works in you who believe.

1 THESSALONIANS 2:13

If the Spirit of Him who raised Jesus from the dead dwells in you, He who raised Christ from the dead will also give life to your mortal bodies through His Spirit who dwells in you.

ROMANS 8:11

Do You Know What to Look For?

The Holy Spirit is doing His work in your life day in and day out. He doesn't need to change a thing. What needs to change is your awareness of His presence and activity. When you know what to look for and when to look for it, you will be amazed at how real the Holy Spirit will become to you.

~

Open my spiritual eyes, dear Lord. Give me the ability to see Your fingerprint on each circumstance of life. Make me cognizant of Your presence.

The Spirit Himself bears witness with our spirit that we are children of God.

ROMANS 8:16

Now He who establishes us with you in Christ and has anointed us is God, who also has sealed us and given us the Spirit in our hearts as a guarantee.

2 CORINTHIANS 1:21–22

In Him you also trusted, after you heard the word of truth, the gospel of your salvation; in whom also, having believed, you were sealed with the Holy Spirit of promise.

EPHESIANS 1:13

You Are Sealed by the Spirit

When you became a Christian, you were sealed into Christ. The term *sealed* is used in various ways throughout the New Testament. In every case the term carries with it the ideas of protection and security. To seal something means to close it off from outside influences and interference.

When God looks at you, He sees the Holy Spirit within you. The presence of the Holy Spirit is a spiritual reminder of God's promise to finish what He has begun in you. As long as you belong to the Father, the Holy Spirit will be there, living in you, signifying His ownership.

~

Thank You for sealing me with Your Holy Spirit, Father. Thank You for the assurance that when You look upon me and see that seal, You are continually reminded that You will complete the work You have begun.

There is therefore now no condemnation to those who are in Christ Jesus, who do not walk according to the flesh, but according to the Spirit. For the law of the Spirit of life in Christ Jesus has made me free from the law of sin and death.

ROMANS 8:1–2

I say then: Walk in the Spirit, and you shall not fulfill the lust of the flesh. For the flesh lusts against the Spirit, and the Spirit against the flesh; and these are contrary to one another, so that you do not do the things that you wish.

GALATIANS 5:16–17

It's What You Do

The immediate result of walking by the Spirit is not discovering which job to take, which person to marry, or which car to buy. The immediate result is that you will not carry out the desires of the flesh.

This is such a positive approach. Instead of being told what not to do, we are given positive direction that will result in avoiding things we have no business involving ourselves in.

The Spirit-filled life is not a life of "don'ts"; it is a life of "dos." Do walk in the Spirit, and you will avoid fulfilling your sinful desires.

~

I want to walk in Your Spirit, dear Lord. I realize if I do, I won't have to worry about the "don'ts." Make me sensitive to the promptings of Your Spirit.

For Christ also suffered once for sins, the just for the unjust, that He might bring us to God, being put to death in the flesh but made alive by the Spirit.

1 PETER 3:18

If we live in the Spirit, let us also walk in the Spirit.

GALATIANS 5:25

And such were some of you. But you were washed, but you were sanctified, but you were justified in the name of the Lord Jesus and by the Spirit of our God.

1 CORINTHIANS 6:11

How Will You Respond?

Spirit-filled men and women are not isolated from what's going on around them. And they are not without their faults. They experience hurt and disappointment like everybody else. They have their daily bouts with temptation.

What sets them apart from the rest of the world is their response. When circumstances wreak havoc with the peace of Spirit-filled people, there will be some down time. But they won't stay down. They refocus their attention on the big picture, acknowledge the truth that their peace is from the Lord, and then move on.

~

I want to respond properly, heavenly Father, but I need Your help! Take my disappointment and sorrow, the failures of my flesh. Rechart my spiritual course to walk in Your Spirit.

He said to them, "Follow Me."

MATTHEW 4:19

Jesus said to His disciples, "If anyone desires to come after Me, let him deny himself, and take up his cross, and follow Me."

MATTHEW 16:24

If anyone serves Me, let him follow Me; and where I am, there My servant will be also. If anyone serves Me, him My Father will honor.

JOHN 12:26

Set Your Mind on Spiritual Things

The Holy Spirit is committed and equipped to guide you. He will guide you according to truth. But He will not override your will and force you to follow. You have a part to play. And it begins with your mind.

It is essential that you remain surrendered because walking by the Spirit involves following. You can't follow and lead at the same time.

To walk by the Spirit is to live with moment-by-moment dependency on and sensitivity to the initial prompting of the Holy Spirit. It is a lifestyle.

~

You lead, and I will follow, Father. You are already my life, but I want to make walking in Your Spirit my lifestyle. Let me begin today.

For to be carnally minded is death, but to be spiritually minded is life and peace.

ROMANS 8:6

If anyone is in Christ, he is a new creation; old things have passed away; behold, all things have become new.

2 CORINTHIANS 5:17

That you put off, concerning your former conduct, the old man which grows corrupt according to the deceitful lusts.

EPHESIANS 4:22

You Can Change

The Holy Spirit is a change agent. Change is what He is all about. He took a man who made his living destroying churches and changed him into the greatest church planter of all time! He took a group of uneducated fishermen and changed them into world-class evangelists and pastors. Through the years He has indwelt men and women with every imaginable habit, reputation, and persuasion and changed them into people of excellence. And He will do the same for you.

Your part is to plug into the new life that indwells you.

~

Change me, Lord. Radically. Definitely. Substantively. I don't want a patched-up version of my old self. I want to be a new creature in Christ.

STRENGTHENING YOUR FAMILY RELATIONSHIPS

For he who is called in the Lord while a slave is the Lord's freedman. Likewise he who is called while free is Christ's slave.

1 Corinthians 7:22

Whatever you do, do it heartily, as to the Lord and not to men, knowing that from the Lord you will receive the reward of the inheritance; for you serve the Lord Christ.

Colossians 3:23–24

Ask What You Can Do

If you are not sure how to love your family, try serving them. One of the most famous quotes from the era of President John F. Kennedy had to do with service in this statement: "Ask not what your country can do for you; ask what you can do for your country." I would paraphrase that for the husbands and wives of this nation: "Ask not what your husband can do for you; ask what you can do for your husband"; "Ask not what your wife can do for you; ask what you can do for your wife."

How many marriages might be saved if this principle were to be lived out?

~

Give me a servant's heart, dear Lord. Then help me live it out in practical reality in my everyday family life. Teach me to serve.

So I will restore to you the years that the swarming
    locust has eaten,
The crawling locust,
The consuming locust,
And the chewing locust.

JOEL 2:25

He also brought me up out of a horrible pit,
Out of the miry clay,
And set my feet upon a rock,
And established my steps.

PSALM 40:2

Bring my soul out of prison,
That I may praise Your name;
The righteous shall surround me,
For You shall deal bountifully with me.

PSALM 142:7

God Can Make Your Family Work

The One who created the first family is the One who is interested in yours and in mine. The God who adopted you into His forever family knows how to make earthly families work.

Family—one man and one woman united in marriage for life and, if God chooses, children either biological or adopted. We can't change God's ideal. Well, I guess we can. Adam and Eve did. And humankind has been paying the price ever since.

God provided the Cross to break their negative family traditions.

~

I lift my family to You today, dear Lord. You see the broken relationships. You feel the hurts. Father, restore my family and make it work.

Behold, children are a heritage from the LORD,
The fruit of the womb is a reward.
Like arrows in the hand of a warrior,
So are the children of one's youth.

PSALM 127:3–4

Children's children are the crown of old men,
And the glory of children is their father.

PROVERBS 17:6

Your Greatest Treasure

There was once a parent who let his son and daughter play inside a fenced-in yard. They knew the boundaries. And they knew the consequences if they failed to obey and stay within the limits. The father loved the two children, and they brought him more joy than anything in his life. But the two children stepped over the boundaries, suffered severe consequences, and broke the father's heart.

The son's name was Adam. The daughter's name was Eve. The father's name is God. God the Father was the perfect Parent, but His first two kids didn't turn out to be perfect. He understands.

~

There are times when I am tired and exasperated, Lord—I must admit it. But in my heart, how thankful I am for the precious gifts of my children. Teach me to cherish them as You do.

And these words which I command you today shall be in your heart. You shall teach them diligently to your children, and shall talk of them when you sit in your house, when you walk by the way, when you lie down, and when you rise up.

Deuteronomy 6:6–7

All your children shall be taught by the Lord,
And great shall be the peace of your children.

Isaiah 54:13

Your Parenting Skills

Although children are very different, certain general principles apply to each. Here are several habits every parent should develop and incorporate into parenting skills:

First, communicate and demonstrate a genuine interest in what goes on in the lives of your children. Second, love and accept your children unconditionally. Third, set limitations. Fourth, meet the material needs of your children. Fifth, pass along your faith. Sixth, teach them to be wise.

~

Lord, how I long to communicate Your unconditional love to my children. Help me to receive it from You so that I can pass it on to them. Give me wisdom to teach and guide my children in Your ways.

That you may love the LORD your God, that you may obey His voice, and that you may cling to Him, for He is your life and the length of your days.

DEUTERONOMY 30:20

God be thanked that though you were slaves of sin, yet you obeyed from the heart that form of doctrine to which you were delivered.

ROMANS 6:17

Know His will, and approve the things that are excellent, being instructed out of the law.

ROMANS 2:18

Did You Do Your Best?

When our children were growing up, we said two things to them over and over again: "Obey God" and "Always do your best." These two things served as the basis of what we considered excellence in our home. We never worried about how popular our kids were at school as much as we did about whether or not they obeyed God. Grades were never stressed in our home. The question was once again, "Did you do your best?" For our daughter, an A was her best in geometry; for our son, his best was a B.

These two standards for raising children emphasize character development over performance.

~

Teach me to obey, dear Lord, so that I can teach my children obedience. Empower me to do my best so that I can challenge them to do their best.

Wives, submit to your own husbands, as is fitting in the Lord.

COLOSSIANS 3:18

I want you to know that the head of every man is Christ, the head of woman is man, and the head of Christ is God.

1 CORINTHIANS 11:3

Husbands, love your wives, just as Christ also loved the church and gave Himself for her.

EPHESIANS 5:25

Filling Your God-Given Role

God gave each of us a role to fulfill in the home. Dad, you are to love your wife as Christ loved the church. Mom, you are to submit to your husband. To ignore these principles, regardless of what else you do to try to compensate for them, is to set your children up for failure.

You can drag your children to church every time the doors are open. You can read the Bible to them every night of their lives. But, Dad, if you are not loving and leading your wife, and, Mom, if you are not graciously submitting to your husband, more harm is being done than good.

~

It's an awesome responsibility, Lord, guiding the lives of my children. I want to be a role model of Your divine design. I know I can't do it in myself, but I can through the power of the Cross.

It is required in stewards that one be found faithful.

1 CORINTHIANS 4:2

So he called him and said to him, . . . "Give an account of your stewardship."

LUKE 16:2

The LORD said, "Shall I hide from Abraham what I am doing, since Abraham shall surely become a great and mighty nation, and all the nations of the earth shall be blessed in him? For I have known him, in order that he may command his children and his household after him, that they keep the way of the LORD, to do righteousness and justice, that the LORD may bring to Abraham what He has spoken to him."

GENESIS 18:17–19

You Are a Steward

Y ou must view your children as a stewardship from God. That is, they have been placed into
your life by God so that you can raise them
according to His principles to do His will when
they are old enough to understand what that is.
Such an attitude will give you opportunity to
explain why you do some of the things you do as
a parent. It will also help to develop in your children at a young age a sense of personal responsibility to God.

As a steward, you can explain to your children
that you have been given the responsibility to
raise them according to their heavenly Father's
guidelines; you have found through the years that
Father knows best.

~

I am a steward of Your treasures. Thank You for that
privilege, Father. Let me reflect this responsibility to
my children and make them accountable to You.

He who walks with wise men will be wise,
But the companion of fools will be destroyed.

PROVERBS 13:20

A man who has friends must himself be friendly,
But there is a friend who sticks closer than a brother.

PROVERBS 18:24

Make no friendship with an angry man,
And with a furious man do not go,
Lest you learn his ways
And set a snare for your soul.

PROVERBS 22:24–25

Your Friends

The Bible promises you will be affected significantly by people you choose to relate to. You will become wise by associating with those who are wise, or you will suffer the painful consequences of imprudent relationships.

What kind of friends do you have?

You must never sacrifice your relationship with God for the sake of a relationship with another person. If your relationship with God is not primary, you will not be the friend you need to be.

~

Father, help me to step back from negative relationships and draw closer in those that honor You. Be the Lord of all my relationships—including my friendships.

Knowing Your Father's Voice

I will hear what God the LORD will speak,
For He will speak peace
To His people and to His saints;
But let them not turn back to folly.

PSALM 85:8

Therefore My people shall know My name;
Therefore they shall know in that day
That I am He who speaks:
"Behold, it is I."

ISAIAH 52:6

Eli said to Samuel, "Go, lie down; and it shall be, if He calls you, that you must say, 'Speak, LORD, for Your servant hears.'" So Samuel went and lay down in his place. Now the LORD came and stood and called as at other times, "Samuel! Samuel!" And Samuel answered, "Speak, for Your servant hears."

1 SAMUEL 3:9–10

God Wants to Speak to You

God still actively participates in communicating His message to believers today: He loves us just as much as He loved the people of the Old and New Testament days; we need His definite and deliberate direction for our lives as did Joshua, Moses, Jacob, or Noah; and He wants us to know Him.

Today, God speaks to us through His Word, through the Holy Spirit, through other godly people, and through circumstances. When God speaks (and He does), everyone should listen.

~

Father, open my ears to hear You speaking to me through Your Word, the Holy Spirit, other believers, and my circumstances. Attune my ear to hear Your voice.

Your ears shall hear a word behind you, saying,
"This is the way, walk in it,"
Whenever you turn to the right hand
Or whenever you turn to the left.
ISAIAH 30:21

The LORD will guide you continually,
And satisfy your soul in drought,
And strengthen your bones;
You shall be like a watered garden,
And like a spring of water, whose waters do not fail.
ISAIAH 58:11

For You are my rock and my fortress;
Therefore, for Your name's sake,
Lead me and guide me.
PSALM 31:3

Give God Your Attention

When God speaks to us, we must recognize that His message is of utmost importance, deserving our full and complete concentration. Lest we become dull and insensitive to His voice, God has His ways of gaining our undivided attention.

God cares enough to employ various and sundry methods to cause us to stop and listen to what He is saying. He will not let us wander aimlessly through the snarled interchanges of everyday life without pointing us to the appropriate signposts He has already erected. He does so by gently speaking to us.

~

Heavenly Father, let me be attentive and responsive to Your spiritual signposts as they guide me through the snarled interchanges of my daily life. Most important, help me recognize Your stop signs.

I am the good shepherd; and I know My sheep, and am known by My own.

JOHN 10:14

And other sheep I have which are not of this fold; them also I must bring, and they will hear My voice; and there will be one flock and one shepherd.

JOHN 10:16

My sheep hear My voice, and I know them, and they follow Me.

JOHN 10:27

You Will Know His Voice

When we are saved, it is natural, normal behavior to know that when God speaks, it is our Father who has called us by name.

If we as believers walk in the Spirit, understand the meaning of the Cross, and allow the Holy Spirit to fill us and live His life through us, then it should be easy for us to distinguish whether the voice we hear is of God, the flesh, or the devil. The natural walk of Spirit-filled, committed believers is such that when God speaks, we can identify His voice.

~

I want to know when You speak to me, Lord. No doubt. No questioning. No indecision. I want to know my Father's voice.

To him the doorkeeper opens, and the sheep hear his voice; and he calls his own sheep by name and leads them out. And when he brings out his own sheep, he goes before them; and the sheep follow him, for they know his voice. Yet they will by no means follow a stranger, but will flee from him, for they do not know the voice of strangers.

JOHN 10:3–5

God Is Your Intimate Friend

When we hear God, do we listen to an intimate Friend or a distant friend only casually acquainted with us? A distant friend may give ear to our prayers if we happen to be interested in the same things he's concerned about, but an intimate Friend is One who listens, whether or not the subject matter is of great interest. Understanding God as an intimate Friend or as a distant acquaintance influences the degree of openness we have in our conversations with Him.

~

Be my intimate Friend, dear Lord. Walk with me. Talk with me. Let us share together. I need a best Friend.

Trust in the LORD with all your heart,
And lean not on your own understanding;
In all your ways acknowledge Him,
And He shall direct your paths.

PROVERBS 3:5–6

While it is said:
"Today, if you will hear His voice,
Do not harden your hearts as in the rebellion."

HEBREWS 3:15

If you are willing and obedient,
You shall eat the good of the land.

ISAIAH 1:19

You May Not Like What You Hear!

When Jesus came to the Garden of Gethsemane, He was already committed to the Father's will. However, He struggled with the Father to determine whether there was another way to accomplish God's purpose. He struggled with separation from the Father while at the same time He was committed to God's will.

There will be times when we come to God, listen to Him, and then grapple with what we hear. We may be as submissive as we know how at that moment but still wrestle with what He says. Submission must accompany listening if we are to fully hear God.

~

I must admit I don't always like what I hear, dear Lord. Sometimes—like a spoiled child—I want my own way. Although I wrestle sometimes, I really want to obey Your voice. So please, keep speaking.

Oh, how I love Your law!
It is my meditation all the day.
You, through Your commandments, make me wiser
than my enemies;
For they are ever with me.
I have more understanding than all my teachers,
For Your testimonies are my meditation.
I understand more than the ancients,
Because I keep Your precepts.

PSALM 119:97–100

Your Personal Meditations

Many believers think that meditation is only for ministers or other spiritual leaders. They do not see its role in a secular world where strife and competition reign.

God gave the practice of meditation not just to preachers, but to all His children so that we might better relate to Him. Personal, private meditation begins when we get alone with the Lord and get quiet before Him. It may be for five minutes; it may be for thirty minutes; it may be for an hour. The important thing is that we get alone with the Lord to find His direction and purpose for our lives.

~

The noise of this world competes for my attention, Lord. Help me hear Your voice above the din and clatter of my everyday life. Let me learn stillness in Your presence. Let me embrace silence.

Blessed is the man
Who walks not in the counsel of the ungodly,
Nor stands in the path of sinners,
Nor sits in the seat of the scornful;
But his delight is in the law of the LORD,
And in His law he meditates day and night.
He shall be like a tree
Planted by the rivers of water,
That brings forth its fruit in its season,
Whose leaf also shall not wither;
And whatever he does shall prosper.

PSALM 1:1–3

Commit Yourself to Listen

A committed mind is fertile soil. It has been cultivated, ready for the seed to penetrate. It can enclose the seed, envelop the seed, provide the heat and moisture needed for the seed to germinate and bring forth fruit.

We must apply the truths that God impresses in our hearts. And we must make a commitment to obey the truths that God has impressed upon our lives.

It is spiritually impossible to apply the Word week after week and remain the same. As listeners with committed minds, we become productive, maturing children of God.

~

Dear Lord, cultivate the furrows of the soil of my heart, mind, and spirit. Envelop the seed of Your Word with the elements needed to bring forth spiritual fruit. Make me like a tree planted by the rivers of water. Stable. Productive.

Then He said, "Go out, and stand on the mountain before the LORD." And behold, the LORD passed by, and a great and strong wind tore into the mountains and broke the rocks in pieces before the LORD, but the LORD was not in the wind; and after the wind an earthquake, but the LORD was not in the earthquake; and after the earthquake a fire, but the LORD was not in the fire; and after the fire a still small voice.

1 KINGS 19:11–12

His Voice Meets Your Need

Elijah went to Mount Horeb because he knew that was where he could hear God speak. He was not disappointed. A great wind, earthquake, and fire passed in front of Elijah, but there was no speaking voice. Then suddenly a quiet breeze stirred at the mouth of Elijah's cave. In a few brief seconds, God revived the sagging prophet.

So it is that we, as believers, often weary and worried, need to hear just one thing to refresh, encourage, and strengthen us in our service of the King—God's voice.

~

No other voice will meet my need, Father. I must hear from You. One voice. One word to the situations of my life. That's all I need.

She had a sister called Mary, who also sat at Jesus' feet
and heard His word. . . . "But one thing is needed, and
Mary has chosen that good part, which will not be taken
away from her."

LUKE 10:39, 42

Truly my soul silently waits for God;
From Him comes my salvation.

PSALM 62:1

Wait on the LORD;
Be of good courage,
And He shall strengthen your heart;
Wait, I say, on the LORD!

PSALM 27:14

You Can Choose the Good Part

God's total, concentrated, and undisturbed attention is focused upon us individually. That ought to humble us and create within us a reverence that acknowledges God for the mighty Creator He is. Out of the billions of people who make up this universe, God is interested in you.

Like Mary, we should learn to listen to the Lord's Word, seated at His feet. When we do, we can trust that we have chosen that good part, which will not be taken away. For when once we have heard God speak, nothing else compares.

~

Thank You, dear Lord, that You are not too busy for me. You listen daily for my voice. I cherish the privilege of communicating with You. I choose—above all else—to sit at Your feet, to wait in Your presence.

Pursuing

purity

Let us therefore come boldly to the throne of grace, that we may obtain mercy and find grace to help in time of need.

Hebrews 4:16

Enter into His gates with thanksgiving,
And into His courts with praise.
Be thankful to Him, and bless His name.

Psalm 100:4

For He Himself is our peace, who has made both one, and has broken down the middle wall of separation.

Ephesians 2:14

Your Path to Personal Purity

God has gone to great lengths to provide the potential for a lasting relationship with us. He initiated and paid for the entire process. Love for us motivated Him to come up with a plan. And that same love moved Him to sacrifice His Son along the way.

When you sin, you pay Him no tribute by staying away. He has paved the way for you to approach Him immediately after you have sinned. You should take advantage of that. He has reconciled you to Himself. Nothing stands between you. God fixed the incompatibility problem permanently, eternally.

~

Thank You, Father, that the path is clear. I can come boldly into Your presence. Nothing stands between us. There is no incompatibility.

Is this not the fast that I have chosen:
To loose the bonds of wickedness,
To undo the heavy burdens,
To let the oppressed go free,
And that you break every yoke?
Is it not to share your bread with the hungry,
And that you bring to your house the poor who are
    cast out;
When you see the naked, that you cover him,
And not hide yourself from your own flesh?

ISAIAH 58:6–7

164

Your Preparation

Fasting—the biblical discipline of abstaining from food for spiritual purposes—is not a tool to manipulate God to change His mind. There are specific reasons for fasting:

• Fasting prepares us. Fasting provides the opportunity to get away from the negative impact the world has on our decisions and allows us to hear God without outside interference.

• Fasting cleanses. It is a means of personal cleansing for the physical body, ridding it of impurities.

• Fasting equips us for the battle we wage against Satan.

~

Cleanse me, Father. Equip me for the battle with Satan. Prepare my heart to know Your will. Make my personal purity more important than my daily food.

Now all things are of God, who has reconciled us to Himself through Jesus Christ, and has given us the ministry of reconciliation, that is, that God was in Christ reconciling the world to Himself, not imputing their trespasses to them, and has committed to us the word of reconciliation. Now then, we are ambassadors for Christ, as though God were pleading through us: we implore you on Christ's behalf, be reconciled to God.

2 CORINTHIANS 5:18–20

Your Reconciliation

To reconcile something is to make it compatible with something else; it is the process of bringing harmony between two or more things. Theologically speaking, reconciliation is the process by which God made sinful humankind compatible with Himself.

Christ died for everyone, yet not everyone is reconciled to God. Christ's death on the cross paved the way for everyone to be reconciled, but God doesn't force Himself on anyone. It is true that the reconciliation process is God's work from beginning to end, but that process doesn't benefit us until we accept His gift of reconciliation—Jesus Christ.

~

You have reconciled me, dear Lord. How great is this truth! I rejoice in its reality today and exchange my spiritual garments stained by guilt and sin for Your robe of righteousness.

And not only that, but we also glory in tribulations, knowing that tribulation produces perseverance; and perseverance, character; and character, hope.

ROMANS 5:3–4

Let no one despise your youth, but be an example to the believers in word, in conduct, in love, in spirit, in faith, in purity.

1 TIMOTHY 4:12

Your Character

Character is to relationships what oil is to a motor. If you took apart the engine of a new car, you would find that each part was made to work perfectly with all the other parts of that engine. Yet if you run that engine without oil, certain parts of that engine will eventually destroy the parts around them. Why? Friction and heat.

The same is true in relationships. When there is a deficit in character, you pay for it in relationships. It doesn't matter how perfectly suited you are to your spouse, your job, or your club. If you don't have character, there is going to be friction.

~

I don't always do what is right, Lord, but I want to know and do what is right. Lubricate my spiritual engine with the oil of Your Holy Spirit. Let there be no friction.

For they indeed for a few days chastened us as seemed best to them, but He for our profit, that we may be partakers of His holiness. Now no chastening seems to be joyful for the present, but painful; nevertheless, afterward it yields the peaceable fruit of righteousness to those who have been trained by it.

HEBREWS 12:10–11

You have forgotten the exhortation which speaks to you as to sons:
"My son, do not despise the chastening of the LORD,
Nor be discouraged when you are rebuked by Him;
For whom the LORD loves He chastens,
And scourges every son whom He receives."

HEBREWS 12:5–6

Your Behavior

Holiness is being conformed to the image of Jesus Christ. When our behavior fails to align with our true identity in Christ, God disciplines us for our own good. He is willing to bring into our lives whatever is necessary to accomplish that purpose.

Since God is holy, what method does He use to conform us to that image? The method is discipline through training. God is our Father. We are His sons and daughters. The work of the Holy Spirit is to train us, sift and sand us, chip away at things that are foreign to the family we belong to.

~

Conform me to Your image, Father. That is my prayer today. Sift and sand me. Chip away the rough spots. Accomplish Your purpose in my life.

Nevertheless even among the rulers many believed in Him, but because of the Pharisees they did not confess Him, lest they should be put out of the synagogue; for they loved the praise of men more than the praise of God.

JOHN 12:42–43

Peter and the other apostles answered and said: "We ought to obey God rather than men."

ACTS 5:29

So we may boldly say:
"The LORD is my helper;
I will not fear.
What can man do to me?"

HEBREWS 13:6

Your Performance

Seeking the approval of the crowd is uncertain. One day we feel like heroes to everyone. Then we fumble.

Most of the time, people around us don't boo loudly. But they leave us to stand alone. As long as we need the approval of others, we will be condemned to a life of having to always perform perfectly, and not one of us is capable of doing that.

Praise God, we serve One who approves of us unconditionally! We don't have to perform for Him to do so. He confirmed our worth when He sent His Son to die in our place.

~

Thank You, Lord, that I do not have to perform to be accepted. Let the approval or disapproval of the crowd fade in my ears. Attune my spirit to listen for Your confirmation of my true worth.

That good thing which was committed to you, keep by the Holy Spirit who dwells in us.

2 TIMOTHY 1:14

They overcame him by the blood of the Lamb and by the word of their testimony, and they did not love their lives to the death.

REVELATION 12:11

For no other foundation can anyone lay than that which is laid, which is Jesus Christ. Now if anyone builds on this foundation with gold, silver, precious stones, wood, hay, straw, each one's work will become clear; for the Day will declare it, because it will be revealed by fire; and the fire will test each one's work, of what sort it is.

1 CORINTHIANS 3:11–13

Your Testimony

Your character needs to be solid. What you are on the inside is so much more important than what you look like on the outside.

What does your conduct say? Words come easily. A godly walk—or conduct—needs to be maintained and carefully watched over.

Paul told young Timothy to guard the treasure entrusted to him. The treasure was his testimony. If you are a Christian, you have a treasure. It's uniquely yours.

You need to guard your character, your conduct, and your conversation.

~

What a treasure You have entrusted me with, Father! My testimony. Help me guard my character, conduct, and conversation as things of enduring value.

Search me, O God, and know my heart.

PSALM 139:23

Who can understand his errors?
Cleanse me from secret faults.

PSALM 19:12

Wash me thoroughly from my iniquity,
And cleanse me from my sin.

PSALM 51:2

The heart is deceitful above all things,
And desperately wicked;
Who can know it?

JEREMIAH 17:9

Your Hidden Enemies

Enemies are hard to deal with when you can see them. But when they are hidden, they are really difficult.

Paul admonishes us to turn on the lights in our lives and spotlight hidden enemies of love. It's a painful and long process. It's even more painful when you must take part of the blame and say, "I have met the enemy: Me."

Jesus understands how wounded you are. He knows about pain and sorrow.

He just wants to help you in your battle. Let Him.

~

My heart is deceitful, dear Lord. There are things hidden deep within of which I am not even aware. Turn the searchlight of Your Word upon the shadows of my spirit. Let Your light dissipate the darkness.

For "who has known the mind of the LORD that he may instruct Him?" But we have the mind of Christ.

1 CORINTHIANS 2:16

If then you were raised with Christ, seek those things which are above, where Christ is, sitting at the right hand of God. Set your mind on things above, not on things on the earth.

COLOSSIANS 3:1–2

Since Christ suffered for us in the flesh, arm yourselves also with the same mind, for he who has suffered in the flesh has ceased from sin.

1 PETER 4:1

Your Mind

The power of the mind is awesome. It is evident when we realize the mind is the control tower of character, conduct, and conversation. We can think profitably or unprofitably, rightly or wrongly, and the rest of life will be influenced by this thinking. Godly living is the result of godly thinking.

You need to sift your thoughts through the Word of God to the will of God. You need to ask, "What does the Word of God say?"

~

Thank You, Father, that I have the mind of Christ. Sift my thoughts through the screen of Your Word and Your will.

SPENDING TIME WITH GOD

However, the report went around concerning Him all the more; and great multitudes came together to hear, and to be healed by Him of their infirmities. So He Himself often withdrew into the wilderness and prayed.

LUKE 5:15–16

He said to them, "Come aside by yourselves to a deserted place and rest a while." For there were many coming and going, and they did not even have time to eat.

MARK 6:31

Your Quiet Time

A quiet time, or devotion as some prefer to call it, is personal time alone with God. It is a time set aside to talk to and listen to the Father. It is a time we carve out from our busy schedules to give God our undivided attention. I like to think of it as my personal appointment with the heavenly Father.

Christ came to create the potential for intimacy between Him and His people. For that potential to become a reality, we must pursue the relationship through regular time alone with the Father. That is why a devotional life is so significant.

~

Father, increase my desire to spend time with You. I want to know You in intimate, personal relationship. I want to be called Your friend.

Since a promise remains of entering His rest, let us fear lest any of you seem to have come short of it.

HEBREWS 4:1

Behold, I stand at the door and knock. If anyone hears My voice and opens the door, I will come in to him and dine with him, and he with Me.

REVELATION 3:20

This is My beloved Son. Hear Him!

MARK 9:7

Your Appointment with God

If you are serious about developing a consistent devotional life, you must schedule your time with God. Life demands it. Specifically, before you go to bed tonight, you need to have already decided when and where you plan to get alone with the Father.

Personally, I find mornings to be the best time to meet with God. I enjoy getting up early and beginning my day listening to and talking with Him. There is something special about focusing on the Father first thing.

~

Dear Lord, I am serious about developing a consistent devotional life. Help me keep my daily appointment with You. Let it become my priority.

May my meditation be sweet to Him;
I will be glad in the LORD.

PSALM 104:34

When I remember You on my bed,
I meditate on You in the night watches.

PSALM 63:6

I remember the days of old;
I meditate on all Your works;
I muse on the work of Your hands.

PSALM 143:5

My eyes are awake through the night watches,
That I may meditate on Your word.

PSALM 119:148

Making Your Meditation Meaningful

Four principles will guide you into meaningful meditation. These principles are liberating truths that cause you to hear the voice of God in a fresh, liberating, invigorating manner.

First, review the past to see patterns that God has woven into your life.

Second, reflect on God, on His greatness and grace and goodness.

Third, remember God's promises.

Fourth, make requests.

~

Father, thank You for all You have done for me—Your grace and goodness, the loving care You have shown me over the years. Help me focus on You and Your promises instead of myself and my problems.

But those who wait on the LORD
Shall renew their strength;
They shall mount up with wings like eagles,
They shall run and not be weary,
They shall walk and not faint.

ISAIAH 40:31

Rest in the LORD, and wait patiently for Him.

PSALM 37:7

I wait for the LORD, my soul waits,
And in His word I do hope.

PSALM 130:5

Lead me in Your truth and teach me,
For You are the God of my salvation;
On You I wait all the day.

PSALM 25:5

Taking Time for God

When we tell God we don't have time for Him, we are saying we don't have time for life, for joy, for peace, for direction, for prosperity, because He is the Source of all. The essence of meditation is a period of time set aside to contemplate the Lord, listen to Him, and allow Him to permeate our spirits. When we think about how much time we spend in the world, we see how desperately we need to be with Him and regain a biblical perspective.

We live in a hurried and rushed world, and it's not going to slow down. So each of us must ask, How am I going to stay in the rush of it all and hear God?

~

Still the beating of my fearful heart. Calm the tumultuous thoughts of my troubled mind. Slow me down, Lord. Let me learn to wait on You.

Behold, as the eyes of servants look to the hand of their
  masters,
As the eyes of a maid to the hand of her mistress,
So our eyes look to the LORD our God,
Until He has mercy on us.
    PSALM 123:2

For thus says the Lord GOD, the Holy One of Israel:
"In returning and rest you shall be saved;
In quietness and confidence shall be your strength."
But you would not.
    ISAIAH 30:15

Be still, and know that I am God;
I will be exalted among the nations,
I will be exalted in the earth!
    PSALM 46:10

Handling the Pressures of Your Life

The pressures in our lives begin to dissipate when we are secluded, silent, and still before the Lord. God pulls the plug in the pressure tanks of our lives, and our anxieties begin to drain. When we first begin to meditate, our frustration levels are usually at full, but as we focus on Him, the reservoirs of tension empty. Biblical meditation causes something to happen to our spirits, our souls, our emotional beings, and even our human bodies.

We can be tired, weary, and emotionally distraught, but after spending time alone with God, we find that He injects into our bodies energy, power, and strength.

~

I'm not good at handling the pressures of life, Lord. I am tired and weary. I need Your touch to refresh my inner being and energize my mind and spirit. I receive it as I wait in Your presence right now.

Call to Me, and I will answer you, and show you great
and mighty things, which you do not know.

JEREMIAH 33:3

"For My thoughts are not your thoughts,
Nor are your ways My ways," says the LORD.
"For as the heavens are higher than the earth,
So are My ways higher than your ways,
And My thoughts than your thoughts."

ISAIAH 55:8–9

Accepting the Answer to Your Prayers

God answers prayers in one of four ways:

"Yes, child, you may have it."

"No, child, this is not good for you."

"Wait, child, I have something better."

"My grace is sufficient for you."

Nowhere in Scripture does it say that God will give us exactly what we ask for every time. He is sovereign. He has the right to say no according to His infinite wisdom. Oftentimes God is up to something we don't know about.

~

Father, I am sometimes a selfish child. I don't like "no" or "wait" for an answer. Help me, dear Lord, to joyously accept Your response, even when it is not what I expected.

He saw that there was no man,
And wondered that there was no intercessor;
Therefore His own arm brought salvation for Him;
And His own righteousness, it sustained Him.

ISAIAH 59:16

Therefore I exhort first of all that supplications, prayers,
intercessions, and giving of thanks be made for all men,
for kings and all who are in authority, that we may lead
a quiet and peaceable life in all godliness and reverence.
For this is good and acceptable in the sight of God our
Savior, who desires all men to be saved and to come to
the knowledge of the truth.

1 TIMOTHY 2:1–4

Filling Your Role as an Intercessor

The term *intercession* literally means "to come upon," "to meet with," "to come between." To intercede is to stand between God and someone. It is to represent another person's concern to God. An intercessor is a go-between.

According to Scripture, we need to follow some guidelines when we intercede for others. We are to pray from hearts of love and compassion. We must ask the Lord to help us see what others see and feel what they feel. And we must be willing to be part of the answer.

~

Lord, use me to stand in the gap between a dying world and a living Savior. Help me see with Your eyes and feel with Your heart. Let me be Your hands extended, Your love in action.

This Book of the Law shall not depart from your mouth, but you shall meditate in it day and night, that you may observe to do according to all that is written in it. For then you will make your way prosperous, and then you will have good success.

JOSHUA 1:8

Speaking to one another in psalms and hymns and spiritual songs, singing and making melody in your heart to the Lord.

EPHESIANS 5:19

How sweet are Your words to my taste,
Sweeter than honey to my mouth!

PSALM 119:103

Varying Your Routine

One of the most common complaints I hear regarding personal devotions is that after a while they become dry, routine, even boring. God is certainly not boring. And chances are, you are not boring, either. So if spending time with God moves in that direction, the culprit is probably your method. No one method will stay fresh forever. When your devotional life begins to get a little dry, it is time to change your method; modify your routine. You may want to journal your thoughts or read a devotional book.

Remember, this is a relationship. Look for ways to keep it fresh.

∼

Breathe upon me, O God, with the freshness of Your Spirit. Morning by morning, renew Your mercies to me. Touch what is dying with the fresh breath of Your Spirit of life. Stir the embers of my flickering zeal.

INDEX OF SCRIPTURES

About the Author

Dr. Charles Stanley is pastor of the 14,000-member First Baptist Church in Atlanta, Georgia. He is the speaker on the internationally popular radio and television program *In Touch* and is the author of many books, including *The Glorious Journey, The Source of My Strength, How to Listen to God, How to Handle Adversity,* and the In Touch® Study Series.

Dr. Stanley received his bachelor of arts degree from the University of Richmond, his bachelor of divinity degree from Southwestern Theological Seminary, and his master's and doctor's degrees from Luther Rice Seminary. He has twice been elected president of the Southern Baptist Convention.

Books by Dr. Charles Stanley

Eternal Security

The Gift of Forgiveness

The Glorious Journey

How to Handle Adversity

How to Keep Your Kids on Your Team

How to Listen to God

In Touch with God

The In Touch® Study Series

   Advancing Through Adversity

   Becoming Emotionally Whole

   Experiencing Forgiveness

   Listening to God

   Overcoming the Enemy

   Relying on the Holy Spirit

   Talking with God

   Understanding Financial Stewardship

The Reason for My Hope

The Source of My Strength

Winning the War Within

The Wonderful Spirit-Filled Life